TOP CLASS

Vocabulary

Year 3

Now supported with CPD training
For info visit www.johnmurraycpd.co.uk

Hopscotch
A division of MA Education Ltd

John Murray

Published by Hopscotch, a division of MA Education, St Jude's Church, Dulwich Road, London, SE24 0PB
www.hopscotchbooks.com
020 7738 5454

©2016 MA Education Ltd

Written by John Murray

Series designed by Claire Swaffield, Fonthill Creative, 01722 717029

Cover illustration by Sara Anderton
www.catandfoxadventures.com

Illustrations by Emma Turner and Sara Anderton

Associate Publisher: Angela Morano Shaw

ISBN 978 1 909 860 131

All rights reserved. This resource is sold subject to the condition that it shall not, by way of trade or otherwise, be lent, hired out or otherwise circulated without the publisher's prior consent in any form of binding or cover other than that in which it is published and without a similar condition, including this condition, being imposed upon the subsequent purchaser.

No part of this publication may be reproduced, stored in a retrieval system, or transmitted, in any form or by any means, electronic, mechanical, photocopying, recording or otherwise, without the prior permission of the publisher, except where photocopying for educational purposes within the school or other educational establishment that has purchased this book is expressly permitted in the text.

Every effort has been made to trace the owners of copyright of material in this book and the publisher apologises for any inadvertent omissions. Any persons claiming copyright for any material should contact the publisher who will be happy to pay the permission fees agreed between them and who will amend the information in this book on any subsequent reprint.

In the Jungle, original poem by Sue Garnett.
From Everyone a Writer - Year 3, published by Hopscotch.
Copyright MA Education Ltd 2012

Contents Page

Introduction 6

Word Meaning I 8

Word Meaning II 12

Word Families I 16

Word Families II 20

Prefixes 24

Suffixes 28

Compound Words 32

Synonyms 36

Homophones 40

Homonyms 44

Formal English 48

Informal Speech 52

Similes 56

Creative Word Play 60

Introduction

Top Class is a series that endeavours to combine traditional approaches to the teaching and learning of grammar, punctuation and vocabulary with new techniques and activities that support and encourage good learning.

The three core areas have been separated into three distinct books aimed primarily at Key Stage 2. The three books ought to be used in conjunction with each other in order to provide learners with a wider learning environment and for them to understand that these core elements of Literacy work together and are not to be applied in isolation.

Specific elements of the new Key Stage 3 National Curriculum have also been included in order to introduce Key Stage 2 learners to more complex grammatical constructions and vocabulary as they make their transition from attaining National Standard to Mastery in writing.

Each book, one for each Year group in Key Stage 2, aims to promote discussion about specific areas of Literacy and provide experiences and opportunities to use and apply what they have learnt.

The three books are as follows:

- **Top Class – Grammar**
- **Top Class – Punctuation**
- **Top Class – Vocabulary**

Each book contains lessons that develop a 'top-down' approach, allowing learners to see how we use language in context, not simply *when* we use a particular word, punctuation mark or grammatical construct but *how* to use it to its best effect when writing independently.

As such, it actively promotes the core principle that to learn grammar and punctuation well and to extend your personal vocabulary effectively, then you must not only see these particular elements of Literacy within authentic and meaningful context and settings but you must then have the opportunity to apply what you have understood in your own independent writing.

All too often children are taught grammar, punctuation and vocabulary with exercises that aren't rooted within an authentic experience; and, as a result, although they may gain full marks in their exercise books, they often misapply or omit what has been learnt in their own free writing.

The *Top Class* series seeks to address this problem using a three staged approach, each Lesson Plan being structured so that learners are encouraged to investigate and explore the English language; initially with support and guidance from their teacher and fellow peers before being asked to apply what they have learnt as individuals.

Think about...

Before undertaking the Guided activity, learners are asked about what they already know about a particular piece of punctuation or grammatical form and where they might have seen it.

This links directly to the Guided text, again helping learners to view grammar, punctuation and vocabulary in context, housing it so that stronger links can be made with prior learning and personal experiences. This can then be used as a springboard to explore and develop this further in a familiar setting.

For example, when looking at our use of capital letters when writing a proper noun, learners may be asked about why people use an atlas or map before looking at a tourist map of London and considering why place names and famous tourist attractions start with a capital letter.

Guided

This is a shared activity that engages the whole class.

Set within a specific and relevant genre of Literacy, it embeds each particular piece of grammar, punctuation or vocabulary being taught in a focused and meaningful way. Moreover, it invites learners to use this information in order to answer a series of questions that are related to the text itself and then begins to move beyond it.

Each of the three questions asked have been carefully formatted so that valuable practice for the end of *Key Stage 2 English grammar, punctuation and spelling test* can be undertaken throughout each Year group. Marks are also available so that pupils gain practice at providing fuller explanations for those questions where two or three marks are being awarded. Answers are provided on the Lesson Plan.

Independent

This activity can be completed as an individual, with a partner or within a small group.

Each Independent activity within the book is also differentiated at an upper and lower level* and offers teachers a range of practical activities that support learners as they practice what they have learnt in the Guided section.

Differentiated activities can be found on the CD Rom.

Homework

Included in this section is a homework activity that aims to encourage wider learning outside of the classroom to take place. There are two types of homework activities that are provided, each having been designed to help learners discover and engage with grammar, punctuation and vocabulary in the 'real' world:

A] Specific 'closed' questions may be asked in order that research skills, both modern and traditional, can be employed to find a particular answer.

For example: What is the capital city of Denmark? Who was the first man to walk on the moon? When necessary, answers are provided on the Lesson Plan.

B] Wider 'open' tasks are given in order to afford learners the opportunity to explore the world around them and collect examples that are both pertinent and authentic.

For example, learners may be asked to find three examples where a shop's name uses an apostrophe in their local high street.

Extension

This final stage of the learning journey is an important one and underscores the importance of using a 'top-down' approach to the teaching and learning of grammar, punctuation and vocabulary.

Each Extension activity within the book is also differentiated at an upper and lower level.*

Its aim is to encourage children to apply what they have learnt in a meaningful and purposeful way in order to embed their learning.

For example, learners may be asked to write a shopping list when planning a party that will naturally include a colon or use strong adjectives to describe a certain event in a story.

More importantly, it is this *writing for purpose* (rather than to score arbitrary marks or achieve irrelevant ticks in an exercise book) that provides a meaningful opportunity for individuals to engage with the English language and create their own work that uses grammar, punctuation and vocabulary in a way that brings their work to life.

In this way, not only will each learner be encouraged to use particular forms of grammar, punctuation or vocabulary correctly but, essentially, they will gain a strong sense of themselves taking an active role as a writer. It gives them a valuable sense of what it is like to be an author, one who uses grammar not only to improve the quality of their work but also to express themselves as best they can using the written word.

The journey from simply understanding how the English language works to being able to apply that knowledge in order to become a capable and confident writer is a journey that will continue into adulthood and one that, in all truthfulness, never really ends.

However, by providing meaningful activities for both the classroom and beyond, the *Top Class* series can help each and every writer to freely use grammar, punctuation and vocabulary to great effect and support them as they endeavour to bring the written word to life in order to inform, influence and entertain their readers.

Differentiated activities can be found on the CD Rom.

TOP CLASS - Vocabulary - Year 3

Word Meaning I

Think about...
What do you do if you come across a word you don't know?
How might you work it out?
"The bird flew to her _____ to feed her chicks."
What might the missing word be? Why?

Guided

A wicked witch has cast a spell to turn some of the words in this fairy tale into sweets.

Which witch might this be? Why might she have done such a thing? How might you find out what each of these words are and change them back into text in order to save Hansel and Gretel? Is there another book (such as a dictionary) that might help you? How so?

Once done, answer the questions on page 9.

Independent

The witch has cast a spell upon some more fairy tales to stop them being read!

On your own, with a partner or in a small group; complete the task sheet provided to you by your teacher on page 10.

Once finished, cut off the homework task to help you broaden your word knowledge through practical reading within a variety of contexts.

Extension

Extend your personal vocabulary and understanding of specific words. Complete the task sheet on page 11.

If you have one, put any words you find interesting in your Personal Dictionary, together with an example of how it can be used effectively in a sentence.

* Answers available on the CD Rom.

Answers

1 The words, in the correct order are as follows: cloaked, evaporated, wafted, bubbled, cobbled, accepted.

2 Allow for personal response.

3a Thirteen

3b There were 13 people at the Last Supper, where Jesus revealed one of them would betray him. His betrayal and subsequent death, led to the number 13 having a bad reputation in Christian culture.

Homework

- 7 years bad luck

- "Find a penny, pick it up and all day long you'll have good luck."

- "To bring good luck, hang the right way. Hang upside down and luck drains away!"

- Good luck (but not for the rabbit)

Remember...
When we come across a word we don't know, we can sometimes work out what it means by using clues in the rest of the text. It's like being a **reading detective**...the more **clues** we find, the more likely we are to work out what this new word means.

Word Meaning I

The forest, which had ✳ the two children in secrecy for so long, suddenly gave way to the most wondrous of sights. The darkness, the gloom, the fear all ✳ to reveal a house like no other…a house made entirely of gingerbread.

The spicy smell of gingery goodness ✳ through the air with open arms.

"Come closer, come closer," the house whispered.

Lollypop flowers and trees topped with candyfloss grew in the garden. A chocolate fountain ✳ with velvety happiness.

"Come closer, come closer," the house whispered.

A ✳ path of peppermints led to a door decorated with the number thirteen. The warm glow of a fire peered out from behind two large portals, a pair of cat-like eyes staring out towards the two new strangers.

"Come closer, come closer," the house whispered.

The invitation was gladly ✳ .

"Welcome," whispered the house as the door began to open.

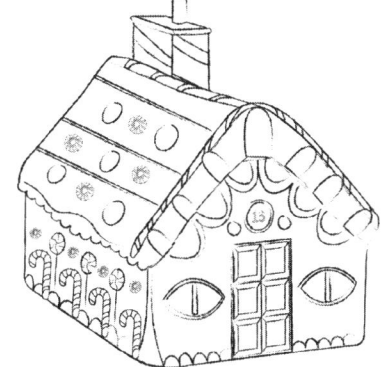

Look at this fairy tale and answer the questions below.

1 Use the six words below to reverse the wicked witch's spell.

cobbled   wafted   cloaked   bubbled   accepted   evaporated

6 marks

2 How did you work out your answers?

_____

_____

_____

3 marks

3a Word Focus:
Find the number that some consider unlucky.

1 mark

3b Word Focus:
Why do many people think this number is unlucky?

3 marks

TOP CLASS - Vocabulary - Year 3

Word Meaning I

A wizard has cast a spell. This spell turns a word into a frog! Read each sentence. Use the clues to work out what each frog is meant to be. Draw and label your answer. Colour the clues that helped you green.

Abracadabra!

Abracadabra, Alikazog. Turn this word here, right into a frog!

The bird flew to her 🐸 to feed her chicks.

The 🐸 galloped over the field and jumped over the fence.

Sam picked up his 🐸 and began to text.

Ajaz knocked on the 🐸 but nobody was in.

Daisy forgot to put a 🐸 on the letter before she posted it.

Everybody sang "Happy 🐸" as Billy blew out the candles.

Dad burnt the 🐸. So we just had a glass of milk for breakfast.

"Who's there?" I whispered as I hid under the 🐸 covers.

Homework

Read about superstitions. What happens if you...
- Break a mirror?
- Find a penny?
- Hang up a horseshoe?
- Carry a rabbit's foot?

Vocabulary

Revisit the text on page 9. Answer each question below.
Highlight the words you explore in the text itself.
Think of ways in which you can learn each one.
Can you act it out or draw it?
Does it remind you of a word you already know? Why?
How will you use your new words in the future?

Name: **Date:**

Underline the root in the following word.

cloaked

Who might wear one of these?

Why do you think the author uses the phrase **'cloaked in secrecy'**?

Draw a **'cobbled'** path.

Is the word **'gloom'** positive or negative?

(+)   (−)

What does this word suggest about the forest?

How strong was the smell of gingerbread?

Not strong   Very strong

1   2   3   4   5

Which word suggests this?

How did this smell travel through the air?

☐ Slowly and gently

☐ Quickly with great force

Which word tells us this?

Which number is used in the text that is often seen as unlucky and suggests something bad will happen next?

Which of these two words means **'to look for a long time with eyes wide open, especially when surprised or when thinking'**?

| To peer | To stare |

How is the other different?

TOP CLASS - Vocabulary - Year 3

Word Meaning II

Think about...
What do you do if you come across a word you don't know? How might you work it out?
"The witch flew away on her _____."
What might the missing word be?
Why do you think this?

Guided

A banshee has spirited away words to stop you from being able to read.

How might you work out what each of the missing words might be? How can you check if the word you have chosen is correct? Why might somebody else have chosen a different word to you and both of you be correct?

Once done, answer the questions on page 13.

Independent

Be a Reading Detective and work out the missing words.

On your own, with a partner or in a small group; complete the task sheet provided to you by your teacher on page 14.

Once finished, cut off the homework task to help you broaden your word knowledge through practical reading within a variety of contexts.

Extension

Extend your personal vocabulary and understanding of specific words. Complete the task sheet on page 15.

If you have one, put any words you find interesting in your Personal Dictionary, together with an example of how it can be used effectively in a sentence.

*Answers available on the CD Rom.

Answers

1 The words, in the correct order are as follows: hag, cloak, shatter, comb, owl, night.

2 Allow for personal response.

3a nocturnal

3b An owl and a bat.

Homework

- Bad luck will visit you
- Good luck will visit you
- You will struggle with money and never be rich
- You will wet the bed

Remember...
When we come across a word we don't know, we can sometimes work out what it is by using clues in the rest of the text. It's like being a **reading detective**...the more **clues** we find, the more likely we are to work out what this new word is.

Word Meaning II

THE BANSHEE

In Irish folklore, a banshee is an evil fairy, an old ___ who dresses in either black or white and wears a dark grey _____.

This terrifying creature shrieks her unholy wails whenever someone is about to die; a wail so piercing it can _____ glass.

She tries to tame her wild hair by brushing it with a silver comb. And it is for this reason, according to the old wife's tale, that should you ever see a _____ lying on the ground, you must never pick it up. For the banshee (having placed it there to lure unsuspecting humans to their doom) will return and spirit you away!

Obviously banshees do not really exist, but one possible explanation as to the origin of this wicked wretch is the high pitched screech of the barn ___ - a nocturnal hunter known for its silent flight and chilling cries in the dead of _____.

Look at this folklore and answer the questions below.

1 Use the six words below to restore the text the banshee has stolen.

    owl   **cloak**   **comb**   **hag**   **night**   **shatter**

6 marks

2 How did you work out your answers?

_____

_____

3 marks

3a Word Focus:

Find a word that describes an animal that hunts at night.

1 mark

3b Word Focus:

Draw two flying creatures that you would describe using this word.

3 marks

Word Meaning II

The wizard is up to his old tricks. This spell turns a word into a bat! Read each sentence. Use the clues to work out what each bat is meant to be. Draw and label your answer. Circle the clues that helped you black.

Hocus Pocus!

Hocus Pocus, Babikazat. Turn this word here, right into a bat!

It was muddy so Farmer Giles put on his 🦇 boots.

"I'm sooooo tired," 🦇 Peter.

It was dark. Magdi struck a match and lit a 🦇.

Mum combed Lucy's 🦇 after swimming.

The 🦇 pulled into the station. "All aboard!" cried the driver.

Tim threw down his book. The last 🦇 was missing! "I'm phoning the library," he huffed.

Black coffee, one sugar please. I don't drink 🦇.

The birds sang and the bees 🦇. Spring was here at last!

Homework

Read about more superstitions. What happens if...
* A black cat crosses your path?
* You find a four-leaf clover?
* You are given an empty purse as a present?
* You pick a dandelion?

Vocabulary

Revisit the text on page 13. Answer each question below.
Highlight the words you explore in the text itself.
Think of ways in which you can learn each one.
Can you act it out or draw it?
Does it remind you of a word you already know? Why?
How will you use your new words in the future?

Name: **Date:**

Draw and label a '**banshee**'.

Which word does the author use to describe '**an ugly old woman**'? Draw your answer.

What type of cry is a '**shriek**'?

Loud	Quiet
High	Low
Short	Long

How is a '**shriek**' different to a '**wail**'?

If a creature is '**nocturnal**' when does it hunt?

Draw and label your answer.

Which synonym does the author use instead of '**evil**' in the final paragraph?

How scary is something that is '**terrifying**'?

Scary   *Very Scary*

1   2   3   4   5

Which words below are family words?
horror   terror   horrible   terrible

Is a '**screech**' a positive or negative sound?

(+)   (−)

| High | Low |
| Long | Short |

TOP CLASS - Vocabulary - Year 3

Word Families 1

Think about...
Look at the following words:
childish actor magic children act magical child reaction magician
Match the words that relate to each other.
Circle the root word.

Guided

You are reading an email between friends.

Do you think this email will be formal or informal? Why? What do you see in this email to show that this is the case? Make a list with your teacher. It is often said friends are the family that you choose. What do you think this means? Do you agree or disagree with this statement? Why? How good a friendship do you think Charlotte, Nic and Ben have? Why do you think this?

Once done, answer the questions on page 17.

Independent

Consider the root meaning of different words.

On your own, with a partner or in a small group; complete the task sheet provided to you by your teacher on page 18.

Once finished, cut off the homework task to help you broaden your word knowledge through practical reading within a variety of contexts.

Extension

Extend your personal vocabulary and understanding of specific words. Complete the task sheet on page 19.

If you have one, put any words you find interesting in your Personal Dictionary, together with an example of how it can be used effectively in a sentence.

*Answers available on the CD Rom.

Answers

1 musical

2 victorious

3a re

3b rewrite, retell, recycle, review, recall, return.

The attachment is on the CD Rom

Homework

- No specific answers are required for this homework, though teachers may find it useful to refer to aspects such as audience, purpose and setting when focusing on the formality of language and highlighting how language changes depending upon whom the reader might be and why it is being written.

Remember...
When we understand the **root** of a word, then we can begin to understand how different words that use the same root relate to each other. Learning **word families** is a great way to extend your word knowledge and appreciate where words come from.

Word Families I

Inbox (37)
Drafts
Sent
Spam (12)
Trash

To: charlotte@talktalk.net
Re: **Ben's Birthday Party**
📎 Musical Chairs

Hi Charlotte,

Really sorry but I can't make Ben's birthday party on Saturday. I'm full of a cold so won't be able to give you a lift! ☹

Can I ask you a huge favour? Can you take Ben's card and present for me?

He's also asked me to send him instructions on how to play Musical Chairs and to lend him a CD player. His Internet is down so if you could take this too, I'd be grateful. ☺☺☺

You'll need to open the instructions and print them off!

Let me know when you can pick up the stuff and save me some cake. I hear it's great for soothing a sore throat! You can fill me in with all the gossip too, LOL. ☺

Cheers big ears,

Nic ☺

Look at the email and attachment and answer the questions below.

1 Find the family word to 'music' in the email.

1 mark

2 Find the family word to 'victor' in the attachment.

1 mark

3a Word Focus:

Find the prefix in the attachment that means 'to do again'.

1 mark

3b Word Focus:

Add the same prefix to the words below.

write   tell   cycle
view   call   turn

What does each new word mean?

3 marks

TOP CLASS - Vocabulary - Year 3   17

Word Families I

Who went to Ben's party? Were they a boy or a girl?
Write their name formally and informally.
What did they enjoy doing at the party?
Underline the root in both their name and their activity.
Write about who did what at the party.

Friends & Family!

Formal	Informal	Activity:	Ben's Party Guests:
Chri<u>st</u>opher	Chris	pl<u>ay</u>ing	Christopher ✓
		singing	Peter
		running	Josephine
		laughing	Matthew
		watched	Nicola
		drinking	Patrick
		listening	Isabella
		chased	Samuel
		joked	Simon
		eating	Phillip

Example: *Chris loved playing football at the party.*

Homework

Read the names on your class register.
Are they written formally or informally? Why?
When and how would you write each of your classmates' names informally?
Are there any names that are hard to shorten? Why?

Vocabulary

Revisit the text on page 17. Answer each question below.
Highlight the words you explore in the text itself.
Think of ways in which you can learn each one.
Can you act it out or draw it?
Does it remind you of a word you already know? Why?
How will you use your new words in the future?

Name: **Date:**

Which two informal words are used in the e-mail? To say hello = _____ To say thank you = _____	Find a synonym that means '**very big**' in paragraph two.
Draw two chairs '**facing**' each other.	Find a formal word in Step 1 that means '**put**'. Is this word a verb or a noun? | Verb | Noun |
What does the phrase '**give you a lift**' mean in the first paragraph? ☐ To help you with a job ☐ To take you somewhere in the car	Find a formal word in Step 4 that means '**take away**'. Is this word a verb or a noun? | Verb | Noun |
Which two words in the set of instructions use a prefix that means '**to do again**'?	Find a word in paragraph three that means '**to give someone something for a short time before they give it back to you**'.

TOP CLASS - Vocabulary - Year 3

Word Families II

Think about...
Look at the following words:
music beauty light musical beautiful lightning musician beautician delightful
Match the words that relate to each other.
Which is the root word? Why do you think this?

Guided

You are reading about dogs that help us.

What do you already know about this subject? Make a list with your teacher of how dogs help us in different ways and the breeds of dogs associated with each idea. Your teacher might show you a picture of each breed of dog…do you know which breed it is?

Once done, answer the questions on page 21.

Independent

Consider the root meaning of different words.

On your own, with a partner or in a small group; complete the task sheet provided to you by your teacher on page 22.

Once finished, cut off the homework task to help you broaden your word knowledge through practical reading within a variety of contexts.

Extension

Extend your personal vocabulary and understanding of specific words. Complete the task sheet on page 23.

If you have one, put any words you find interesting in your Personal Dictionary, together with an example of how it can be used effectively in a sentence.

*Answers available on the CD Rom.

Answers

1 aid, assist

2 Formal – canine
Informal – pooch

3a daily

3b Every week – weekly
Every month – monthly
Every year – yearly, annually

Discuss the fact that not all dogs are friendly and helpful, some bite!

Homework

- She was the first animal to go into space

- On the streets of Moscow (as a stray)

- She died from over-heating in her rocket (Sputnik 2) November 3rd, 1957

- On April 11th, 2008, a monument was unveiled in her honour in Moscow

---

Remember...
When we understand the **root** of a word, then we can begin to understand how different words that use the same root relate to each other. Learning **word families** is a great way to extend your word knowledge and appreciate where words come from.

Word Families II

 Dogs

Not all dogs are lovable pets. Some work hard to aid people in their daily lives, while others work tirelessly in more dangerous situations. Have you ever tried teaching your pooch to roll over, fetch a newspaper or to give you its paw? Then you will know how long this can take and how frustrating it can be.

Here are two breeds of dog that do just that:

Golden Retriever

Often used to assist blind and partially sighted people, this dog is also known for its friendly and placid nature. Although intelligent, they must begin their training as a puppy if they are to learn all the skills they will need to help their owner.

St. Bernard

Known for its strength, this dog rescues climbers from snow covered mountains following a climbing accident or an avalanche. Even when buried deep beneath the snow, with a keen sense of smell and powerful paws, help is never too far away from those in peril.

Little wonder our canine companions are called *man's best friend*!

Look at this factual page and answer the questions below.

1 Find two words that mean 'to help'.

2 marks

2 Find a formal and informal word for 'dog'.

Formal: Informal:

2 marks

3a Word Focus:

Find a word that means 'every day'.

1 mark

3b Word Focus:

Which word would you use to describe...

Every week:
Every month:
Every year:

3 marks

TOP CLASS - Vocabulary - Year 3

Word Families II

Look at each job.
Draw an icon for each one.
Can you spot the root word at the start of each job?
Can you think of any more words related to the root?
Make a list.

We Are Family!

Job		Root	Family Word	People who help us:
magician	✨	magic	magical	magician ✓
				gardener
				artist
				baker
				postman
				teacher
				sailor
				cashier
				electrician
				writer

Homework

Read about a dog called *Laika*.
• Why is this dog famous?
• Where was she found?
• Why didn't she return home?
• How is she honoured today?

Vocabulary

Revisit the text on page 21. Answer each question below.
Highlight the words you explore in the text itself.
Think of ways in which you can learn each one.
Can you act it out or draw it?
Does it remind you of a word you already know? Why?
How will you use your new words in the future?

Name:	Date:
Find a word in the introduction that means **'to get'**.	Find a word under the Golden Retriever heading that means **'to help'**.
If you work **'tirelessly'** how do you think you work? ☐ With lots of energy, without stopping ☐ Slowly because you are tired Why do you think this?	Which word can you spot at the start of the following word? **partially** Does this mean that **'partially sighted'** people can see? Everything Something Nothing at all
What do you think the word **'placid'** means? ☐ Very calm and still ☐ Very excited, with lots of energy Why do you think this?	What happens in an **'avalanche'**? Draw and label your answer.
Which word in the final paragraph means **'someone who travels with you and is a friend'**?	Find an adjective in the introduction that means **'making you feel cross because you cannot do something'**.

Prefixes

Think about...
Look at the following words:
like   true   honest   tie   loyal
kind   connect   pack   well   appear
Are these words positive or negative?
What prefix might you add to make its opposite form?

Guided

You have just woken up and are reading the morning paper. The date is April 15th, 1912.

Is the headline positive or negative? When did this event take place? What is the name of the ship that has sunk? Why was it so famous? Why did it sink? Where did it sink? How many people survived? How many people did not?

Once done, answer the questions on page 25.

Independent

You are learning how to turn positive words into their negative form.

On your own, with a partner or in a small group; complete the task sheet provided to you by your teacher on page 26.

Once finished, cut off the homework task to help you broaden your word knowledge through practical reading within a variety of contexts.

Extension

Extend your personal vocabulary and understanding of specific words. Complete the task sheet on page 27.

If you have one, put any words you find interesting in your Personal Dictionary, together with an example of how it can be used effectively in a sentence.

*Answers available on the CD Rom.

Answers

1 Unsinkable

2 Unhappy, disappear, unfriendly, disagree, disloyal, unwise.

3a long, deep

3b wound (This word is a homograph so it is important that it is pronounced correctly, the intonation of the voice going downwards to ensure the word is recognised as a noun. If pronounced wrongly, this word becomes a verb: *she wound up the clock*).

Homework

- No specific answers are required for this homework, though teachers may wish to invite learners to present their research about their chosen Titanic passenger in either written or spoken form. Passenger boarding tickets could be pulled from a hat to ensure that each learner has a different passenger or crew member to research. This will help ensure that a variety of Titanic stories will be told.

Remember...
A **prefix** is found at the start of a word. We use some prefixes such as '**un**' and '**dis**' to turn a positive word into its negative form.

Prefixes

"Great Loss of Life"
So read one London headline reporting the tragic sinking of the *Titanic*.

On the night of April 14th, 1912, the biggest and most luxurious ocean liner of its time hit an iceberg.

A gash measuring over 90 metres long ripped along her side, puncturing six of the watertight compartments that had been designed to keep her afloat.

No ship could survive such a wound. Her fate was sealed!

With many passengers and crew believing the ship to be "unsinkable" (and with only enough lifeboats to save 1178 people) reactions were slow. Many lifeboats were launched before they were even full.

And what a great loss of life it was too!

Of 2201 people on board only 712 were rescued by the *Carpathia*.

The rest perished in the icy Atlantic waters, lost forever to the watery depths.

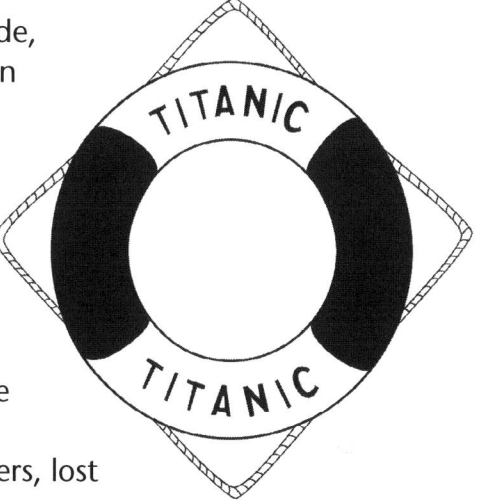

Look at this report and answer the questions below.

1 Which word uses a negative prefix in a positive way?

1 mark

2 Add the negative prefix 'un' or 'dis' to the following words:

happy   **appear**   **friendly**

agree   **loyal**   **wise**

3 marks

3a Word Focus:

Draw a gash.

What type of cut is a gash?

1 mark

3b Word Focus:

Which word links to this idea in paragraph four?

How would you say this word out loud?

3 marks

TOP CLASS - Vocabulary - Year 3

Prefixes

Look at the words below. Which prefix does each use to turn it into its negative form?
Colour the 'un' words blue and 'dis' words red.
Which words can use both? Colour these boxes yellow.
Choose three negative words from each column.
Put them in a sentence of your own.

You're So Negative!

Un	Root Words	Dis
	lucky wrap agree	
	appear lock obey	
	usual honest kind	
	tidy connect known	
	cover respectful fair	
	well like fit count	
	courage safe allowed	
	approve	

Homework

Research a passenger on board the *Titanic*.
- Who were they?
- Where were they from?
- What did they do while the ship was sinking?
- Did they survive?

Vocabulary

Revisit the text on page 25. Answer each question below. Highlight the words you explore in the text itself. Think of ways in which you can learn each one. Can you act it out or draw it? Does it remind you of a word you already know? Why? How will you use your new words in the future?

Name: **Date:**

What do we call a group of people who work on a ship? Draw and label your answer.

What do we call a group of people who have paid to travel on a ship? Draw and label your answer.

Would something '**luxurious**' cost you a lot of money?

| Yes | No |

Is a story that is '**tragic**' happy or sad?

Sad   *Happy*
    1   2   3   4   5

Can you think of a tragic event you have seen in the news recently?

What does the word '**great**' mean in the title?

☐ Fantastic

☐ Large number

☐ Famous

Find a formal word in the last paragraph that means '**died**'.

_____

How formal is this word?

Formal   *Very formal*
    1   2   3   4   5

Find a word in paragraph five that means '**to put a boat or ship into water for the first time**'.

What type of cut is a '**gash**'?

| Long | Short |
| Deep | Shallow |

Would it bleed a little or a lot?

TOP CLASS - Vocabulary - Year 3

Suffixes

Think about...
Look at the following words:
**young strong brave wise
pretty hungry big thin**
Add 'er' or 'est' to each word.
What rules do you notice?

Guided

You are exploring the mysterious Red Planet.

Which planet do you think we will be looking at? Why? What do you already know about this planet? Is there anything you don't know about this planet and would like to find out? Write your question on a post-it note and give it to your teacher. How might you find the answer to your question?

Once done, answer the questions on page 29.

Independent

You are investigating comparatives and superlatives.

On your own, with a partner or in a small group; complete the task sheet provided to you by your teacher on page 30.

Once finished, cut off the homework task to help you broaden your word knowledge through practical reading within a variety of contexts.

Extension

Extend your personal vocabulary and understanding of specific words. Complete the task sheet on page 31.

If you have one, put any words you find interesting in your Personal Dictionary, together with an example of how it can be used effectively in a sentence.

Answers

1 I. smaller
II. longer

2 largest

3a A mnemonic is anything (usually a simple rhyme) that helps you remember something else.

3b Allow for personal response.
For example:
laugh **a**bout **u**gly **g**irls' **h**air

Homework

- Jupiter (nearly 11 times bigger than Earth)
- Mercury (nearly 2.5 times smaller than Earth)
- Jupiter (equivalent to around 318 Earths)
- Saturn (this planet would float in water because it is so light)

Remember...
A **suffix** is found at the end of a word. When we add **'er'** to some words we turn it into a **comparative word** and when we add **'est'** we turn it into a **superlative word**.

Suffixes

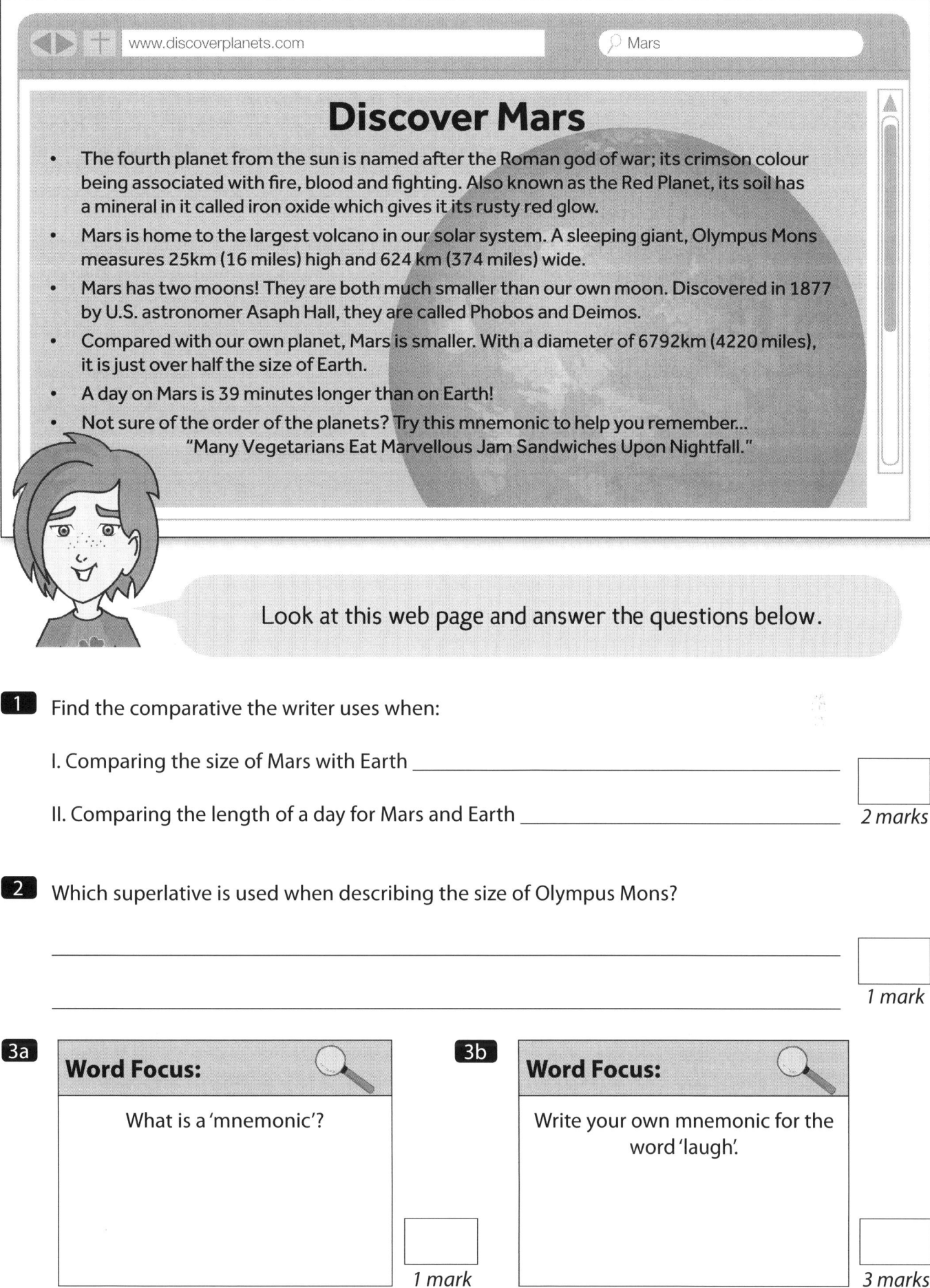

Discover Mars

- The fourth planet from the sun is named after the Roman god of war; its crimson colour being associated with fire, blood and fighting. Also known as the Red Planet, its soil has a mineral in it called iron oxide which gives it its rusty red glow.
- Mars is home to the largest volcano in our solar system. A sleeping giant, Olympus Mons measures 25km (16 miles) high and 624 km (374 miles) wide.
- Mars has two moons! They are both much smaller than our own moon. Discovered in 1877 by U.S. astronomer Asaph Hall, they are called Phobos and Deimos.
- Compared with our own planet, Mars is smaller. With a diameter of 6792km (4220 miles), it is just over half the size of Earth.
- A day on Mars is 39 minutes longer than on Earth!
- Not sure of the order of the planets? Try this mnemonic to help you remember...
 "Many Vegetarians Eat Marvellous Jam Sandwiches Upon Nightfall."

Look at this web page and answer the questions below.

1 Find the comparative the writer uses when:

I. Comparing the size of Mars with Earth _____

II. Comparing the length of a day for Mars and Earth _____

2 marks

2 Which superlative is used when describing the size of Olympus Mons?

_____

1 mark

3a Word Focus:

What is a 'mnemonic'?

1 mark

3b Word Focus:

Write your own mnemonic for the word 'laugh'.

3 marks

Suffixes

Add **er** or **est** to each root word.
Which is the comparative? Which is the superlative?
Investigate how we do this.
Write a rule to explain how we do this.
Write a short story using some of these new words in it.

Comparatives & Superlatives:

Rule 1:

Rule 2:

Root Words:

slow large hot ugly fast

wet brave lucky strong

safe thin pretty rich fierce

sad scary

Rule 3:

Rule 4:

Homework

Read about the planets in our Solar System.
- Which planet is the biggest?
- Which planet is the smallest?
- Which planet is the heaviest?
- Which planet is the lightest?

30   TOP CLASS - Vocabulary - Year 3

Vocabulary

Revisit the text on page 29. Answer each question below.
Highlight the words you explore in the text itself.
Think of ways in which you can learn each one.
Can you act it out or draw it?
Does it remind you of a word you already know? Why?
How will you use your new words in the future?

Name: **Date:**

What colour is '**crimson**'? Colour your answer.

Which is the word '**solar**' related to?

The sun   The moon

Colour your answer.

What is an '**astronomer**'?

_____

_____

Check your answer in a dictionary.

Why do you think the author uses the word '**discovered**' and not '**found**'?

_____

_____

_____

Why do you think the word '**discover**' is also used in the title?

_____

_____

_____

What do '**vegetarians**' not eat?

☐ Vegetables

☐ Meat

Why do you think this?

Why does the author call Olympus Mons a '**sleeping giant**'?

_____

_____

_____

What measurement is a '**diameter**'?

_____

_____

What is the diameter of this circle?

TOP CLASS - Vocabulary - Year 3

Compound Words

Think about...
Join the following words to 'snow':
man   flake   ball
Add a word to begin each of these words:
ball   print   path
What do we call these new types of words?

Guided

You are considering how and why people create compound words.

Why do you think people in the past created compound words to describe something new? Do you think this was a good or bad idea? Why? Can you think of any examples of your own?

Once done, answer the questions on page 33.

Independent

You are looking at ways in which compound words are created.

On your own, with a partner or in a small group; complete the task sheet provided to you by your teacher on page 34.

Once finished, cut off the homework task to help you broaden your word knowledge through practical reading within a variety of contexts.

Extension

Extend your personal vocabulary and understanding of specific words. Complete the task sheet on page 35.

If you have one, put any words you find interesting in your Personal Dictionary, together with an example of how it can be used effectively in a sentence.

*Answers available on the CD Rom.

Answers

1 Verse 1 [1]: lighthouse
Verse 2 [3]: pathway, signpost, torchlight
Verse 3 [0]
Verse 4 [2]: snowflakes, footprints
Verse 5 [2]: outstretched, heartfelt

2 Light/house, path/way, sign/post, torch/light, snow/flakes, foot/prints, out/stretched, heart/felt.

3a A lot

3b growling, howling. Allow for personal response.

Homework

- Rachel Green, Monica Geller, Phoebe Buffay, Joey Tribbiani, Chandler Bing and Ross Geller.

- New York

- 22nd September, 1994

- The Rembrandts

Remember...
A **compound word** is made by joining two smaller words together.

Compound Words

Friendship

When the waves are high and the seas are rough,
When the rocks are jagged and times are tough,
You are my anchor, my lighthouse, my friend.

When the sun is setting and the light grows dim,
When the pathway fades and darkness creeps in,
You are my signpost, my torchlight, my friend.

When a storm is approaching and the wolf is a growling,
When rain lashes down and the wind is a howling,
You are my shelter, my refuge, my friend.

People come and go through life,
Like snowflakes in your hand.
When trouble's near, they disappear,
Like footprints in the sand.

But you my friend are here for me,
Through thick and thin you'll stay.
An outstretched hand, a heartfelt word,
To guide me on my way.

Look at this poem and answer the following questions.

1 How many compound words are in each verse? List them.

_____
_____ *5 marks*

2 Write each example in a box below. Draw a line to show where the two words have come together.

[ ] [ ] [ ] [ ]
[ ] [ ] [ ] [ ] *4 marks*

3a Word Focus:
When rain 'lashes down' is it raining a little or a lot?

Draw your answer. *1 mark*

3b Word Focus:
List two words the poet uses that links to a wolf.

[ ] [ ]

Why does the poet link a wolf with bad weather? *3 marks*

TOP CLASS - Vocabulary - Year 3

Compound Words

Cut out each set of words. Mix them up and place face down. Take turns to turn over two words. If you make a compound word, you keep it. If you don't, put your two words back. The player with the most compound words at the end of the game is the winner.

news + paper = newspaper

Word beginnings:

wind	tooth	star	key
motor	rain	sun	eye
moon	foot	news ✓	black
butter	green	snow	water
cup	post	under	some

Word endings:

bow	house	where	light
fly	box	ache	berry
hole	board	man	way
mill	paper ✓	sight	fall
fish	flower	ground	ball

Homework

Read about the T.V. series *Friends*.
- List the six main characters.
- Where was the series set?
- When was the first episode shown?
- Who sang the theme tune?

Vocabulary

Revisit the text on page 33. Answer each question below.
Highlight the words you explore in the text itself.
Think of ways in which you can learn each one.
Can you act it out or draw it?
Does it remind you of a word you already know? Why?
How will you use your new words in the future?

Name: **Date:**

How dangerous are '**jagged**' rocks?

Safe   *Dangerous*

1   2   3   4   5

Why?
_____

Draw an anchor.

What does an anchor do?

How does darkness '**creep**' in?

Quickly	Slowly
Quietly	Noisily

If the light is '**dim**', how bright is it?

Very dark   *Very bright*

1   2   3   4   5

If the rain '**lashes**' down, how hard is it raining?

A little   *A lot*

1   2   3   4   5

Draw your answer.

If your words are '**heartfelt**' what are they like?

Warm   Cold   Kind

Unkind   Loving   Harsh

Truthful   Untruthful

Why would you hold your hand '**outstretched**'?
_____
_____
_____

When something '**fades**', how does it do it?

Quickly	Slowly
All of a sudden	Gradually

TOP CLASS - Vocabulary - Year 3

Synonyms

Think about...
Which is your favourite season?
Why do you like it so much?
Look at the following two words:
Beautiful   Lovely
How are they similar? How are they different?

Guided

You are reading a story with a twist!

What is a twist? Does a twist usually happen at the start or the end of a story? Why are these types of stories so memorable? Do you like stories that end with a twist? Why? Why not?

Note: Teachers may wish to discuss the aspect of what a twist is after reading the text so as not to spoil the twist itself.

Once done, answer the questions on page 37.

Independent

Consider how and why writers use synonyms.

On your own, with a partner or in a small group; complete the task sheet provided to you by your teacher on page 38.

Once finished, cut off the homework task to help you broaden your word knowledge through practical reading within a variety of contexts.

Extension

Extend your personal vocabulary and understanding of specific words. Complete the task sheet on page 39.

If you have one, put any words you find interesting in your Personal Dictionary, together with an example of how it has been used effectively in a sentence.

*Answers available on the CD Rom.

Answers

1 towered, colossal, enormous, gigantic

2 gigantic + enormous (ginormous)

3a banquet, feast

3b A 'trek' is a long walk, usually over mountains and through forests. The phrase 'short trek' is playing with the reader – The distance travelled may be short to us but would be much longer and harder for a tiny ant. Indeed, small hills would be like mountains, grass like a thick forest.

Homework

- Robert Wadlow (USA)
- He reached 8 feet 11.1 inches (272 cm)
- Zeng Jinlian (China)
- She reached 8 feet 1.75 inches (248.3 cm)

Remember...
A **synonym** is a word that has a similar meaning to another. However, there are no true synonyms in the English language. Every word has its own unique meaning. We must understand the shades of meaning a word has if we are to use it correctly and to its greatest effect.

Synonyms

The Picnic

It was a glorious day. Primrose Park beckoned; an army, after all, marches on its stomach.

A short trek to Honeysuckle Hill and they had arrived at their destination.

They weren't disappointed.

A baby blue blanket sprawled out under a large oak tree; an empty hamper sat nearby. A grand feast lay before them, a banquet fit for a Queen...and her workers!

To the north: a skyscraper of jam sandwiches towered above them. To the south: a colossal stack of sausage rolls piled high. To the east: an enormous salad bowl of deliciousness. To the west: a gigantic chocolate cake smothered in heavenly butter cream.

And best of all, the ginormous creatures known as "humans" were far too busy playing Frisbee to notice that their lunch was under attack and quickly making its way towards another little hill called home.

Look at this story and answer the questions below.

1 Reread paragraph five. List the four words that mean 'very big'.

4 marks

2 Which two words have come together to create the word 'ginormous'?

2 marks

3a Word Focus:
Find two words in paragraph four that tell us there was a lot of food.

1 mark

3b Word Focus:
What is odd about the phrase 'short trek'?

Why do you think the author wrote this phrase?

3 marks

Synonyms

Find the synonyms for the word 'big'. There are eight examples altogether. However, it is important we know when to use each one. When you have found all eight, put each one into a sentence of your own.

Word Search:

C	L	M	A	S	S	I	V	E	T
A	H	U	G	E	I	R	E	S	R
G	I	G	A	N	T	I	C	A	E
F	M	F	I	O	E	L	O	J	M
A	M	E	S	R	D	E	L	X	E
T	E	R	K	M	O	S	O	S	N
F	N	V	R	O	E	D	S	I	D
E	S	A	A	U	R	I	S	A	O
L	E	O	V	S	E	H	A	P	U
P	Y	J	O	Y	T	K	L	I	S

BIG

colossal

huge

enormous

gigantic

vast

tremendous

immense

massive

Example: *The pirates sailed across the vast ocean.*

Homework

Read about real giants: *www.thetallestman.com*
- Who was the tallest man to have lived?
- How tall was he?
- Who was the tallest woman to have lived?
- How tall was she?

Vocabulary

Revisit the text on page 37. Answer each question below.
Highlight the words you explore in the text itself.
Think of ways in which you can learn each one.
Can you act it out or draw it?
Does it remind you of a word you already know? Why?
How will you use your new words in the future?

Name:	Date:
"It was a **glorious** day" What does this word tell us about the weather? _____ _____ _____	What type of walk is a '**trek**'? 	A long walk	A short walk	 	An easy walk	A difficult walk	
Colour the blanket '**baby blue**'.	Find two words in paragraph four that link with food. |_____|_____| What do these two words tell us?
What is another name for a basket used to carry food in?	Which part of your body do you use to '**beckon**' somebody? Show your teacher how to '**beckon**' somebody.
Why do you think the author uses the word '**towered**' when describing the sandwiches? _____ _____ _____	How much butter cream was on the cake? **A thin layer** **A thick layer** **On the top** **On the sides** **Everywhere** What word tells us this? _____

TOP CLASS - Vocabulary - Year 3

Homophones

Think about...
Look at the following words:
**flower wear hare night pear
knight pair hair flour where**
Which would you pair up? Why?
How is each word different in meaning?

Guided

You are researching the water cycle and come across some weather jokes:

1. What did Santa's wife say to him during a thunderstorm? Come look at the rain, dear.
2. What do you call the weather if it's raining chickens, ducks and geese? Fowl!

Which joke did you like best? Why? How did the punchline make you laugh?

Once done, answer the questions on page 41.

Independent

Consider how some words that sound the same but are spelt differently possess different meanings.

On your own, with a partner or in a small group; complete the task sheet provided to you by your teacher on page 42.

Once finished, cut off the homework task to help you broaden your word knowledge through practical reading within a variety of contexts.

Extension

Extend your personal vocabulary and understanding of specific words. Complete the task sheet on page 43.

If you have one, put any words you find interesting in your Personal Dictionary, together with an example of how it has been used effectively in a sentence.

*Answers available on the CD Rom.

Answers

1

weather	whether
missed	mist
rain	reign
son	sun

2 Allow for personal response.

3a droplet (+let = small)

3b piglet, owlet, booklet, leaflet, eaglet

Homework

- No specific answers are required for this homework. This exercise is best undertaken as a class over a longer period of time. It also affords you the opportunity to make practical links with Numeracy when discussing how to measure the weather in terms of temperature (°C), rainfall (mm) and the strength of the wind (mph).

Remember...
A **homophone** is a word that sounds the same as another but is spelt differently and has a different meaning.

Homophones

A cloud is a large collection of tiny water droplets.
When water on Earth evaporates, it turns into water vapour. The higher into the sky it rises the cooler the air around it becomes. This causes the water vapour to condense and form a cloud.

There are three main types of clouds:

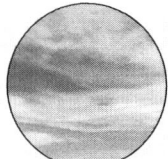 **Cirrus**
These clouds are seen very high in the sky. They are white and wispy. Because they are so thin, the sun shines through them. If you see these clouds you can predict fair to pleasant weather.

 **Cumulus**
These form in the middle of the sky. Usually white and puffy they look like floating cotton. However, as they grow they become heavier and darker, bringing with them the possibility of heavy rain, thunderstorms, snow and hail.

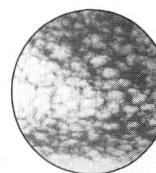 **Stratus**
These hang low in the sky. Flat and grey they cover the whole sky in a dull, dreary uniform. Light mist and drizzle sometimes falls from these clouds.

Look at the encyclopaedia page and answer the questions below.

1 Which of the following homophones are used correctly in this text?

weather	whether	rain	reign
missed	mist	son	sun

4 marks

2 Write a sentence for each of the words you have chosen.

_____

_____

4 marks

3a **Word Focus:**
Which word ends with a suffix that means 'very small' in paragraph one.

1 mark

3b **Word Focus:**
How do the following words use this suffix to mean 'small'?

pig   owl   book

leaf   eagle

3 marks

TOP CLASS - Vocabulary - Year 3

Homophones

Match two homophones from the box below.
Write each pair of words on a domino.
Draw two different pictures on each domino to show what each different homophone means.
Can you make some dominoes of your own?

Sounds Good to Me!

| night | pear | see | sun | nose | meat | eight | deer | wait | Wales | leek | write |
| ate | son | wails | meet | pair | sea | right | knight | dear | weight | knows | leak |

Homework

Keep a weather diary.
- What was the weather like yesterday?
- What was the average temperature?
- How much rainfall was there?
- How fast was the wind blowing?

Vocabulary

Revisit the text on page 41. Answer each question below.
Highlight the words you explore in the text itself.
Think of ways in which you can learn each one.
Can you act it out or draw it?
Does it remind you of a word you already know? Why?
How will you use your new words in the future?

Name: **Date:**

On a scale of 1-5, how small is a '**droplet**' of water?

Tiny *Huge*

1   **2**   **3**   **4**   **5**

Why do you think this?

What happens when water '**evaporates**'?

_____

_____

_____

Use a dictionary to help you.

Is '**vapour**' a solid, a liquid or a gas?

solid   liquid   gas

Use a dictionary to help you.

When water vapour '**condenses**', how does it change?

☐ From a liquid into a gas

☐ From a gas into a liquid

Check your answer in a dictionary

When you '**predict**' something, what do you do?

☐ Describe what will happen *before* the event

☐ Describe what has happened *after* the event

When would you predict the weather for?
Today   Tomorrow   Yesterday

Is the word '**dull**' positive or negative?

(+)   (-)

What colour are the clouds likely to be?

_____

Is the word '**dreary**' positive or negative?

(+)   (-)

How are you likely to be feeling?

Happy   Excited   Unhappy   Bored

If everything is '**uniform**', how do they look?

☐ Everything looks the same

☐ Everything looks different

Is this why you have a school uniform?
Yes   No

TOP CLASS - Vocabulary - Year 3

Homonyms

Think about...
Draw two pictures for each word:
fly   light   ring
watch   bat   head
What do we call these types of words?
What else do you notice?

Guided

Your class reader is the children's classic The Wonderful Wizard of Oz.

What do you already know about this story? Do you think the Wizard is good or bad? Why do you think this? What type of place do you think Oz is? What makes you think this? Do you think it is important to read stories from other countries? Why? Why not?

Once done, answer the questions on page 45.

Independent

Consider how some words that are spelt the same and sound the same have more than one meaning.

On your own, with a partner or in a small group; complete the task sheet provided to you by your teacher on page 46.

Once finished, cut off the homework task to help you broaden your word knowledge through practical reading within a variety of contexts.

Extension

Extend your personal vocabulary and understanding of specific words. Complete the task sheet on page 47.

If you have one, put any words you find interesting in your Personal Dictionary, together with an example of how it has been used effectively in a sentence.

*Answers available on the CD Rom.

Answers

1 A friendship.

2 A group of people.

3a He rested it upon his shoulder, usually with the head of the axe facing downwards.

3b Emerald (green)
Sapphire (blue)
Ruby (red)

Homework

Based on the classic 1939 release:

- 25th August, 1939 (USA)
  11th December, 1939 (UK)

- Judy Garland

- Margaret Hamilton

- Lyman Frank Baum

Remember...
A **homonym** is a word that sounds the same and is spelt the same as another but has a different meaning.

Homonyms

THE WONDERFUL WIZARD OF OZ
CHAPTER 5 – THE RESCUE OF THE TIN WOODMAN

The Tin Woodman gave a sigh of satisfaction and lowered his axe, which he leaned against the tree.

"I might have stood there always if you had not come along," he said; "so you have certainly saved my life. How did you happen to be here?"

"We are on our way to the Emerald City to see the Great Oz," she answered, "and we stopped at your cottage to pass the night."

"Why do you wish to see Oz?" he asked.

"I want him to send me back to Kansas, and the Scarecrow wants him to put a few brains into his head," she replied.

The Tin Woodman appeared to think deeply for a moment. Then he said:

"Do you suppose Oz could give me a heart?"

"Why, I guess so," Dorothy answered. "It would be as easy as to give the Scarecrow brains."

"True," the Tin Woodman returned. "So, if you will allow me to join your party, I will also go to the Emerald City and ask Oz to help me."

"Come along," said the Scarecrow heartily, and Dorothy added that she would be pleased to have his company. So the Tin Woodman shouldered his axe and they all passed through the forest until they came to the road that was paved with yellow brick.

Look at this children's classic and answer the questions below.

1 Find the word 'company'. What does it mean?

- A business ☐
- A friendship ☐

1 mark

2 Find the word 'party'. What does it mean?

- A celebration ☐
- A group of people ☐

1 mark

3a Word Focus:

When the Tin Woodman 'shouldered' his axe, where did he put it?

Act it out.

1 mark

3b Word Focus:

What colour are the following gems?

Emerald   Sapphire   Ruby

3 marks

TOP CLASS - Vocabulary - Year 3   45

Homonyms

Choose a homonym from the list below.
Think of two meanings for each example.
Draw a picture in each circle, one for each meaning.
Is the word a verb or a noun?

It All Sounds The Same To Me!

pants

fly

ring

left

bat

break

watch

box

Homework

Read about the film *The Wizard of Oz*.
- When was the film first released?
- Who played the lead character of Dorothy?
- Who played the Wicked Witch of the West?
- Who wrote the original book the film is based upon?

Vocabulary

Revisit the text on page 45. Answer each question below.
Highlight the words you explore in the text itself.
Think of ways in which you can learn each one.
Can you act it out or draw it?
Does it remind you of a word you already know? Why?
How will you use your new words in the future?

Name: **Date:**

What colour is an emerald?

Colour in your answer.

What type of house did the Tin Woodman live in?

Draw and label your answer.

What two words help make the word '**scarecrow**'?

What material is the Scarecrow likely to be made from?

_____

What does the word '**party**' mean in paragraph nine?

☐ A celebration

☐ A group of people

Circle the root word in:

shouldered

How does the Tin Woodman carry his axe?

Act it out.

Was the Tin Woodman's '**sigh of satisfaction**' positive or negative?

(+)   (-)

Act it out.

How does the Scarecrow say "**come along**"?

_____

Does this mean he said these words:

Loudly   Quietly   With lots of energy
Excitedly   Bored   With no energy

Which word in the title suggests this story is magical and strange?

Magical: _____

Strange: _____

Very good: _____

TOP CLASS - Vocabulary - Year 3

Formal English

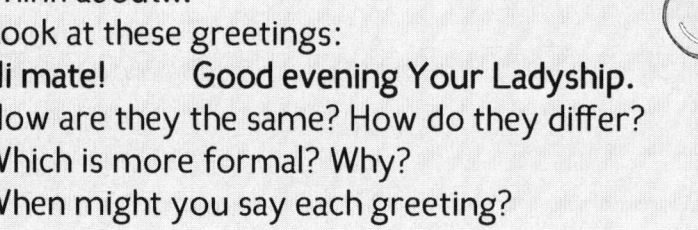

Think about...
Look at these greetings:
Hi mate!   Good evening Your Ladyship.
How are they the same? How do they differ?
Which is more formal? Why?
When might you say each greeting?

Guided

You are visiting the country Manor of Lord and Lady Mulberry.

What might you wear? How would you act? How would you speak when greeting them? How would this differ if you were meeting your best friend after school? Why would this be the case? In what other situations might we want to use more formal language? Why is this important?

Once done, answer the questions on page 49.

Independent

You are comparing the formality of words.

On your own, with a partner or in a small group; complete the task sheet provided to you by your teacher on page 50.

Once finished, cut off the homework task to help you broaden your word knowledge through practical reading within a variety of contexts.

Extension

Extend your personal vocabulary and understanding of specific words. Complete the task sheet on page 51.

If you have one, put any words you find interesting in your Personal Dictionary, together with an example of how it can be used effectively in a sentence.

*Answers available on the CD Rom.

Answers

1 May I ask

2 occur

3a required

3b witness

Homework

- Agatha Christie
- The Mysterious Affair at Styles
- 21st January 1921
- Belgium

Remember...
We use **formal language** when we do not know the person we are talking to. It shows them respect. We also use it when what we are saying is important or the situation we are in is serious.

Formal English

Setting:	The study. The wind is blowing the curtains. Lady Mulberry walks over and closes the window.
Inspector Doyle:	This must have come as a shock. Would you like a seat?
Lady Mulberry:	No, I'm fine. I'd rather stand. I didn't sleep well last night so if I sit down I'll probably fall asleep.
Inspector Doyle:	May I ask, where were you between the hours of midnight and 7am this morning?
Lady Mulberry:	In bed of course. Apart from when I went to the kitchen.
Inspector Doyle:	The kitchen?
Lady Mulberry:	I required a glass of water. I had a headache and wanted to take some tablets.
Inspector Doyle:	And at what time did this occur, Your Ladyship?
Lady Mulberry:	It was 4am. I know because I heard the grandfather clock chime as I was running the tap.
Inspector Doyle:	Did anybody witness you there?
Lady Mulberry:	Nobody Inspector. I was quite alone.

Look at this play script and answer the questions below.

1 How does Inspector Doyle show he is very polite when asking his second question?

_____

1 mark

2 What formal word does Inspector Doyle use instead of 'happen'?

_____

1 mark

3a **Word Focus:**

Find a formal word for 'needed'.

1 mark

3b **Word Focus:**

Find a formal word for 'see'.

Use this word in a sentence of your own.

3 marks

TOP CLASS - Vocabulary - Year 3

Formal English

Lady Mulberry uses very formal language. Her cook uses informal language. Which character would use each phrase? When and where might they do so? Which would you use? When? Who would you use it with? Why?

Key: Lady Mulberry = blue   Cook = yellow

Cheers	Thank you
I received a telephone call yesterday evening.	I got a phone call last night.
Can I ask?	May I enquire?
Do you require any assistance?	Do you need any help?
Give my regards to	Say hi to
I'll need to check that.	I will need to verify that.
Janet	Your Ladyship
I am afraid I cannot answer that Inspector.	I'm sorry I can't answer that.
I'll try my best.	I will endeavour to do my utmost.
That's crazy!	Preposterous!
We ate at 8 on the dot.	We dined at 8 pm precisely.
I regret to inform you.	I'm sorry to tell you.
Don't be stupid!	Ridiculous!

Homework

Read about the famous detective Hercule Poirot.
- Who created this famous detective?
- In which murder mystery did he first appear?
- When was this book first published in the UK?
- Which country is he supposed to come from?

Vocabulary

Revisit the text on page 49. Answer each question below.
Highlight the words you explore in the text itself.
Think of ways in which you can learn each one.
Can you act it out or draw it?
Does it remind you of a word you already know? Why?
How will you use your new words in the future?

Name: **Date:**

What time is midnight?

What do you think '**mid**' is short for in this word?
_____

Is '**shock**' a positive or negative feeling?

(+)   (-)

Does it usually happen quickly or slowly?

Quickly   **Slowly**

What two words make up the word '**headache**'?

Can you think of any more compound words that describe pain like this?
_____

What is the job title of Mr Doyle?
_____

What does the word '**inspect**' mean?
_____
_____

What two words make up the word '**grandfather**'?

What does this suggest about the clock?

It is short   **It is tall**
It is modern   **It is old**

What word does the author use instead of '**ring**'?
_____

What does this suggest about the ringing sound?
_____
_____

Can you spot the number in the following word?

alone

What does the word 'alone' mean?
_____

What formal word does the Inspector use instead of '**see**'?

Informal Speech

Think about...
Put these in order of formality:
Dear Peter   Hi Pete
Dear Mr P. Murray
What might you be writing?
How might you end each text type?

Guided

You have just received a postcard.

What would you expect to find in it? Make a short list of its features with your teacher. How formal would this be? Who might have written it? Why? What sorts of things might it talk about? How do you think it will start and end?*
Why should we use informal language when writing postcards?

Compare this with the formality of writing the address.

Independent

Consider how and why we use informal language when writing to friends and family.

On your own, with a partner or in a small group; complete the task sheet provided to you by your teacher on page 54.

Once finished, cut off the homework task to help you broaden your word knowledge through practical reading within a variety of contexts.

Extension

Extend your personal vocabulary and understanding of specific words. Complete the task sheet on page 55.

If you have one, put any words you find interesting in your Personal Dictionary, together with an example of how it has been used effectively in a sentence.

*Answers available on the CD Rom.

Answers

1 Hi

2 There are eight contractions found in this postcard: you'll, it's, isn't, we've, I've, I'd, we're, I'm

3a **U**nidentified **F**lying **O**bject

3b **L**augh **O**ut **L**oud

Homework

- No specific answers are required for this homework. However, teachers should look out for the use of contracted speech and the appropriate use of the apostrophe. Shortened forms of names and colloquial terms may also be considered, as well as how to start and end informal emails to a close friend.

Remember...
We use **informal language** when we write to our friends and family because it is warm and friendly. Often what we are writing about is fun. However, if we do not know the person or what we are talking about is serious or important, then we must use **formal language** instead.

Informal Speech

Hi Xog,
You'll never guess where I am...Earth!
It's not like Xartopia at all. The water isn't purple for a start – how bizarre is that?
We've cloaked the ship (Earthlings call them UFOs lol) and disguised ourselves. No more green skin for us! I've chosen to be a pink skin with spikey blonde hair; Xanthia has opted for a darker skin and an Afro. She looks amazing! I wish I'd chosen that now.
We visited a small island called Britain yesterday. They speak a funny language called English. I think they learnt it from one of the bigger islands called America or Australia. It seems they're ruled over by a woman called Queen. She must be important...her face is everywhere!
We were going to go to a land called Wales today but mum saw a banner that showed it was guarded by a monster called Dragon so we're going to Scotland instead...far less dangerous.
Dad looked up how we should dress and says we need to wear something called a kilt but I'm not wearing a skirt for anyone!
Wish you were here, Xatalia xxx

Mr X. Avian
175 Orbital Way
Xurgol Province
Xartopia
X24 8PE

Look at this postcard and answer the questions below.

1 What informal word is used instead of 'Dear'?

1 mark

2 Informal contractions are used to join two words together to make a single word using an apostrophe. How many can you find?

4 marks

3a **Word Focus:**
What does the acronym **U.F.O.** stand for?

1 mark

3b **Word Focus:**
What does the acronym **LOL** stand for?

1 mark

Informal Speech

You are writing an email to your best friend. However, it's far too formal! Highlight the parts you think you should change. Rewrite your email so that it's warm and friendly.

Inbox (1)
Drafts
Sent
Spam
Trash

To: david@talktalk.net
CC:
Subject: **RE: Wish you were here**

Dear David,

We are having a brilliant time! It beats school any day.

Steven wants to build sand castles before we come home, but mother said we would not be able to until she had bought more sun cream. Father bought him some armbands for the pool instead. He looks funny. I am glad I do not need to wear them anymore.

Have you ever tried paella? It is really easy to make and does not take long to cook either. It tastes delicious! I will show you how to make it when we return.

You will be glad to know we get back on Friday. I have a surprise for you … you will not be disappointed!

Jennifer is planning a barbeque on Saturday. Would you like to come?

Yours sincerely,

Homework

You have just received an email from your best friend who is returning from holiday very soon. Write a quick reply to their email apologising for not being able to go on holiday with them but that you are looking forward to catching up with them at the BBQ on Saturday.

Vocabulary

Revisit the text on page 53. Answer each question below.
Highlight the words you explore in the text itself.
Think of ways in which you can learn each one.
Can you act it out or draw it?
Does it remind you of a word you already know? Why?
How will you use your new words in the future?

Name: **Date:**

Is **Xartopia** the name of an alien or a planet? Draw your answer.	Is **Xanthia** the name of an alien or a planet? Draw your answer.
What hair colour does **Xatalia** have? Draw, colour and label your answer.	What type of hair does **Xanthia** have? Draw, colour and label you answer.
Underline the root in the following word: **cloaked** What does this tell us about the ship? | It was visible	It was invisible		What planet do '**Earthlings**' come from? Draw and label your answer. Why do you think this? _____
What does the word '**bizarre**' mean? _____ _____ _____ Use a dictionary to help you.	Draw the '**banner**' for Wales that mum saw.

TOP CLASS - Vocabulary - Year 3   55

Similes

Think about...
Look at the branches of a tree in winter.
How might you describe them?
Write out your sentence and share it.
Did you use 'like' or 'as' in your work?
How does this affect the reader?

Guided

You are considering how and why writers use similes.

What is a simile? Why do you think authors use them to describe something? Do you think this is a good or bad thing? Why? Your teacher will now show you something. Describe it using a simile. Show a partner and compare your simile with theirs. Which do you both like best? Share your creative sentence with your class.

Once done, answer the questions on page 57.

Independent

You are looking at ways in which similes are created and what effect they have on the reader.

On your own, with a partner or in a small group; complete the task sheet provided to you by your teacher on page 58.

Once finished, cut off the homework task to help you broaden your word knowledge through practical reading within a variety of contexts.

Extension

Extend your personal vocabulary and understanding of specific words. Complete the task sheet on page 59.

If you have one, put any words you find interesting in your Personal Dictionary, together with an example of how it can be used effectively in a sentence.

*Answers available on the CD Rom.

Answers

1 As quick as lightning.

2 As light as a feather.

3a Verb

3b The beanstalk was alive and moved like a snake. It was dangerous.

Homework

- No specific answers are required for this homework, though the class diary should be kept in a prominent place and both new and more familiar similes be considered generally throughout the year rather than just during a single isolated lesson or unit of work.

Remember...
A **simile** compares one thing with another. It often uses the words '**like**' or '**as**' when doing so. For example:
His smile was as big as Blackpool Tower.
Her love was like a beautiful flower.

Similes

Fee Fi Fo Fum
I smell the blood of an Englishman.
Be he alive or be he dead,
I'll grind his bones to make my bread!

The air shivered as the giant's words boomed in Jack's ears, his heavy footsteps getting ever closer, ever louder.

Jack raced towards the beanstalk and leapt upon the first branch.

Now Jack, being an adventurous lad, had climbed many trees before. But this was no ordinary tree.

Every time he tried to steady his footing or make firm his grip, the beanstalk would snake itself around Jack's body. No matter where he placed each hand or foot, the vines would coil their way around him and begin to squeeze him tight. He had to think fast.

As quick as lightning, he grasped hold of one of the leaves and tore it from the beanstalk. Gripping it with both hands, he closed his eyes, held his breath and with all his might…jumped!

As light as a feather, Jack landed in the dusty yard of his mother's farm. And there, out of the corner of his eye, he glimpsed an axe.

And without a moment's hesitation, he picked it up and began…to…swing…

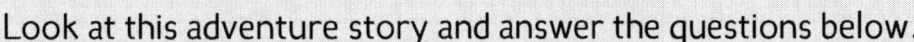

Look at this adventure story and answer the questions below.

1 Which simile is used to describe speed?

_____

_____ *2 marks*

2 Which simile is used to describe how Jack lands?

_____

_____ *2 marks*

3a Word Focus:

Is the word 'snake' in this story a noun or a verb?

1 mark

3b Word Focus:

What does the use of this word tell us about the beanstalk?

3 marks

Similes

Read the beginnings of some well-known similes. Match them to their correct ending and draw a picture cue to help you remember it. When done, put your simile into a sentence. Create two new similes of your own too.

Similes:

as old	as wise	as gentle
as stubborn	as strong	as tough
as clear	as sick	as warm
as busy	as brave	as quiet ✓

as mud	as a bee	as an owl
as a lion	as old boots	as a lamb
as a parrot	as toast	as an ox
as the hills	as a mule	as a mouse ✓

Example: *Jason was <u>as quiet as a mouse</u>. He never said a word at the party.*

Homework

Keep a class diary.
You will see and hear similes being used all the time: in songs, adverts, books…they are everywhere! Write them down. Share them. Draw a picture to remind you what it means and use them in your own stories.

Vocabulary

Revisit the text on page 57. Answer each question below.
Highlight the words you explore in the text itself.
Think of ways in which you can learn each one.
Can you act it out or draw it?
Does it remind you of a word you already know? Why?
How will you use your new words in the future?

Name: **Date:**

Why do you think the air '**shivered**'?

☐ Because it was cold

☐ Because it was scared

Act it out.

How loud was the giant's voice?

Quiet — 1 2 3 4 5 — Very loud

What word tells us this?

How fast did Jack run to the beanstalk?

Slow — 1 2 3 4 5 — Fast

What word tells us this?

Find the word '**snake**'.
How would you classify this word?

| Verb | Noun |

Find two more words in paragraph five that suggest this snaking movement.

| | |

Act both words out.

Which of the following two words means '**to take hold of something quickly**'?

| grasp | grip |

Act it out.

Which of the following two words means '**to hold something very tightly**'?

| grasp | grip |

Show your teacher.

What do you think the word '**glimpsed**' means?

_____
_____
_____

Check your answer in a dictionary.

TOP CLASS - Vocabulary - Year 3

Creative Word Play

Think about...
Look at the following words:
buzz hiss pop hum fizz
Say them out loud.
What do you notice?
What special name do we give these words?

Guided

You are looking at onomatopoeic words.

Write your own definition of what you think these types of words are. Share it with a partner. How is it similar? How is it different? Between you, do you want to rewrite your definition or choose one that sums up both your ideas best? Can you think of any more of these special words? Make a list with your teacher.

Note: Onomatopoeia is when a word's pronunciation imitates its sound.

Independent

You are learning about special words often used in poetry called onomatopoeic words.

On your own, with a partner or in a small group; complete the task sheet provided to you by your teacher on page 62.

Once finished, cut off the homework task to help you broaden your word knowledge through practical reading within a variety of contexts.

Extension

Extend your personal vocabulary and understanding of specific words. Complete the task sheet on page 63.

If you have one, put any words you find interesting in your Personal Dictionary, together with an example of how it can be used effectively in a sentence.

*Answers available on the CD Rom.

Answers

1 The sound of the bell being rung as the door opens. This onomatopoeic word suggests a single, small bell is being rung, its ringing sound being high pitched.

2 I. Being written in capitals suggests a loud and big noise, albeit quick and short lived.
II. The exclamation mark emphasises the brief (and shocking) nature of the sound.

3a snortled

3b Allow for personal response.

Homework

- No specific answers are required for this homework. However, performers may wish to consider how they wish to perform their work: as a group, in pairs or alone. Will they use musical instruments or just their voice? Will they move or stand perfectly still? What are the reasons for their choices?

Remember...
When you read **onomatopoeic words**, how you say the word (whether inside your head or out loud) will be the same as how the word sounds.

Creative Word Play

Florence's Florist
Whatever you say, say it with flowers.

Ting-a-ling.

In walked a gentleman. Wearing a navy blue suit and clutching his wallet, his eyes darted around the shop: white lilies, pink carnations, red roses…and there, in a curious corner, was a flower that he had never seen before.

'How much is that plant?' said the man looking at his watch.

'Oh, that's not for sale Sir. It's more of a pet than a plant. I couldn't possibly let it go.'

'What utter nonsense! This is a flower shop, isn't it? You do sell flowers, don't you? I have neither the time nor the patience to play games old woman. Now are you going to allow me to purchase that plant or not?'

The old woman stood perfectly still, her warm smile fading like the morning dew.

The plant began to rustle.

'Perhaps Sir would like to step a little closer and partake of its scent. An unusual fragrance, I'm sure you will agree; an aroma like no other I assure you.'

'Indeed I would,' snortled the man. And as he stepped into the shadows…
SNAP!

In a single gulp, he was gone. Lunch, it seemed, had been served.

Look at this Cautionary Tale and answer the questions below.

1 What sound is being described in line 1?

_____

_____

1 mark

2 Why do you think the author has written the word SNAP!

In capitals: _____

With an exclamation mark: _____

2 marks

3a Word Focus:

Find a nonsense word that describes how the man 'snorted' and 'chuckled' at the same time.

1 mark

3b Word Focus:

Find three words the old woman uses instead of the word 'smell'.

3 marks

TOP CLASS - Vocabulary - Year 3

Creative Word Play

Learn this poem by heart. How will you perform it? Which lines might you whisper? Why? Which would you say loudly? How do you know? Which lines contain onomatopoeic words? Use musical instruments and your voice to enhance your dramatic performance.

In the Jungle by Sue Garnett

Down in the jungle
Down in the jungle
Parrots go squawk
Parrots go SQUAWK!

Down in the jungle
Down in the jungle
Snakes go hiss
Snakes go HISS!

Down in the jungle
Down in the jungle
Monkeys go eeh
Monkeys go EEH!

Down in the jungle
Down in the jungle
Tigers go roar
Tigers go ROAR!

Down in the jungle
Down in the jungle
Run for your life
RUN FOR YOUR LIFE!

Homework

Write some more verses to Sue's jungle poem. Make sure you copy her rhythm and style so that the poem flows and continues to make sense. Don't forget to use onomatopoeic words to replicate the sounds the jungle makes too!

Vocabulary

Revisit the text on page 61. Answer each question below. Highlight the words you explore in the text itself. Think of ways in which you can learn each one. Can you act it out or draw it? Does it remind you of a word you already know? Why? How will you use your new words in the future?

Name: **Date:**

What colour is '**navy blue**'?

When the gentleman's eyes '**darted**' around the shop, how did they look?

In one part of the shop	All over the shop
Quickly	Slowly

What is the formal name for a flower shop?

When the plant begins to '**rustle**', what sound does it make?

Loud   Quiet   Soft

Deep   Wet   Dry

How hard is the gentleman holding his wallet?

Not very hard   *Very hard*

1   2   3   4   5

Act it out.

What word tells us this?

When the author writes about the old woman's smile '**fading like the morning dew**', does this tell us her smile disappears quickly or slowly?

Quickly	Slowly

Why?

What part of the body do you snort from? Draw and label your answer.

What does the nonsense word '**snortled**' tell us about the man?

What does the word '**curious**' mean?

Check you answer in the dictionary.